Dec 2013

Happy Cooking at FSU

Acknowledgment

*To all the hotels, hostels, inns
and beds-and-breakfasts around the world.
Bless you. Bless you all. I love you all equally.
And I mean that sincerely. Really.*

*Mom
X*

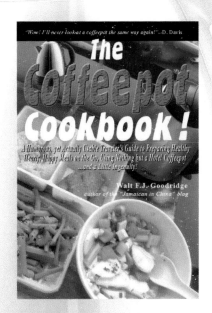

"Wow! I'll never look at a coffeepot the same way again!" -D. Davis

the Coffeepot Cookbook !

A Humorous, yet Actually Usable Traveler's Guide to Preparing Healthy, Hearty, Happy Meals on the Go, Using Nothing but a Hotel Coffeepot ...and a Little Ingenuity!

Walt F.J. Goodridge
author of the "Jamaican in China" blog

D1255611

The Passion Profit Company
a division of a company called W
NEW YORK, SAIPAN, CHINA, LAOS, SINGAPORE

The Coffeepot Cookbook: A Funny, yet Functional and Feasible Traveler's Guide to Preparing Healthy, Happy Meals on the Go Using Nothing but a Hotel Coffeepot.... and a Little Ingenuity

Published and distributed by:
The Passion Profit Company,
a division of a company called W
PO Box 618
Church Street Station
New York   NY 10008-0618
email: orders@coffeepotcookbook.com

Inquiries to the author may be addressed to:
Walt Goodridge
PO Box 503991
Saipan MP 96950
email: walt@coffeepotcookbook.com

Educational institutions, government agencies, libraries and corporations are invited to inquire about quantity discounts.

Retail Cost: $14.23*
ISBN-10: 0983580804   **ISBN-13:** 978-0-9835808-0-5

Printed in the United States of America   First Edition

NOTE: I really wanted to make this cookbook full color AND charge only $12.00, but to do so, would mean I would lose money on every sale. (That would be like ME paying YOU to read my book. How silly!) Then I thought about making the cookbook black and white, but whoever heard of a black and white cookbook????--Walt

TABLE OF CONTENTS

Introduction.
(or, "Why the publishers rejected me")

My original idea was to call this book *The Joy of Coffeepot Cooking* and model it after an obscure "Joy of" book I read a long time ago. However, the major publishers I sent my manuscript to weren't pleased.

NOTHING COMPARES TO

THE JOY OF Coffepot Cooking

Since 2011 more than 8 people have come to this wise, witty, and uninhibited bestselling guide to cooking and found all they wanted to know about achieving greater culinary atisfaction. They have discovered how cooking can be playful and imaginative, erotic and passionate, pleasurable and exhilarating. Now, with this fully revised 2011 edition, The Coffeepot Cookbook promises to captivate an entirely new generation of readers.

Dear Mr. Goodridge,

If we may be so blunt: what on earth were you thinking???

Where on earth did you get the ill-advised notion that you could simply lift the preface to one of the most popular books of the decade and simply overwrite (quite sloppily at that) the word "sex" and "sexual," with "coffeepot cooking" and "culinary," and not think anyone would notice?

Further, why on earth would you think that a respected publisher as we are would encourage such chicanery by even considering it for publication? Please do not send us any manuscripts in the future.

"Necessity is the mother of invention.
Hunger is the father of ingenuity.
The Coffeepot Cookbook is their bastard stepchild."

CHAPTER 1:
Why, where and
what on earth
indeed !

<u>WHY</u> I WROTE THIS BOOK

I wrote this book, fittingly enough, in a hotel room in Hainan, China. It started with a blog post. Actually, it started with the first coffee-pot-cooked meal I prepared in Kunming, China, during the 2010 season of my award-nominated blog, Jamaican in China! (The truth is, nominations are a dime-a-dozen, but even though you know that, you're still impressed, admit it.) Actually, I did place in the five finalists, and, at least one collusion-conspiracy-theorist thinks I actually won, though you didn't hear that from me. But, I digress.

As I said, I was traveling around China from hotel to hotel, and being human in this particular life on earth, I've come to realize that I require sustenance for survival. However, the restaurants across China were not catering to vegan, health fanatics, so I had to devise a strategy for survival that didn't compromise my ethics and dietary guidelines. So, I used a little Jamaican ingenuity and, having nothing but a coffeepot at my disposal, set about cooking what turned out to be a great, healthy meal (see photo below)—at least by my standards.

The historic FIRST coffeepot-cooked meal in Kunming, China

I planned to do a series of blog posts about it (hence the historic photo), but then, in Xishuangbanna—the next stop on my nomad trail—I was fortunate enough to find an apartment with a kitchen. So without necessity or hunger spurring me on, I shelved the idea. But then, on the island of Hainan, China, it was back to hostel rooms with coffeepot as sole amenity, so I had to pull the coffeepot cooking concept out of cold storage, thaw, rehydrate and blog about it! (Yes, there will be similar food/cooking metaphors and puns sprinkled sparingly—there's another one—throughout this book. You have been warned.)

After my first blog post about my Hainan coffeepot experience, D. Davis, a friend and follower of my exploits, uttered (or more accurately, typed) these fateful words, *"Wow! I'll never look at a coffeepot the same way again!"*

Being the astute, finger-on-the-pulse-of-world-mood, and marketing genius I am, I immediately recognized those words as the perfect review, befitting prominent placement right above the title of a book cover. *[Note to D. Davis: Now, obviously, if I named the blog post "Recipes from the Coffeepot Cookbook," I already had the concept of a book in mind. So, don't come looking for any residuals or royalties or any more acknowledgement than you've just received! But thanks!]*

In any event, I wrote this book to share the profound fulfillment and joy that comes from being able to survive and eat healthy meals while seeing the world, by stretching the limits of your creativity and innovating a bit....all on a shoestring budget. And you know what they say about innovation. In the famous words of Larry Ellison (Oracle co-founder, and likely a coffeepot enthusiast himself):

"When you innovate, you've got to be prepared for everyone telling you you're nuts." ~ Larry Ellison

WHERE THIS BOOK MAY LEAD YOU

A second reason I wish to share this information was captured quite eloquently by FDR, who said:

"Never again will we have to fear the spontaneity, minimalism or unpredictability of the backpacker, nomadic life. The only thing we have to fear is THEM taking away our right to..., um, what? Oh, I thought you said "POT cookbook! My bad...."— **Frankie D. Roosevelt** *(the lesser known, less politically inclined great, great grandson of the 32nd President of the US, as quoted in High Times Magazine Belgium supplement)*

What FDR said (parts of it at least, minus the expletives, as he was forcibly removed from the stage at the recent Coffeepot Cooking Convention in Orlando, Florida), remains true. When you're traveling, especially if you're a finicky eater, you don't always have access to your familiar and favorite foods, or trusted brands of condiments. In some cases and countries, you can't even trust the ingredient labels on packaged foods, or the wait staff and chefs (and I use that term generously) at certain restaurants. If you don't want to consume MSG or other chemicals, you'd be wise not to eat in certain restaurants.

However, thanks to *The Coffeepot Cookbook*, you no longer have to fear how you'll survive when you decide to escape the rat race and live a nomad's life, or when you decide to finally purchase your round-the-world ticket and do some country-hopping. Thanks to *The Coffeepot Cookbook*, as long as there's a coffeepot and a produce stand wherever in the world you are, you will be able to dine healthfully!

Note: Coffeepot cooked meals are NOT pre-cooked at home and warmed up in a freezer bag. That type of amateur cooking is easy to do when you're going camping for few days, when you are starting from and returning to the safety and predictability of a home with a kitchen, modern appliances, and a fully stocked pantry. No, Coffeepot Cooking is real cooking for the rugged, spontaneous individualist who doesn't know which rat-infested hell hole of a hotel he'll wind up in tomorrow. These are meals you make <u>from scratch</u> wherever in the world you are—provided there's a coffeepot.

Also, because the Coffee Pot Cookbook is written by a vegan, minimalist, health fanatic (that would be me), you might be introduced to some items that may be new to your palate, but that are quite healthy. Ever tried millet or quinoa? They're two of the healthiest grains out there, and easier to prepare than rice or potatoes. Within these pages, are a selection of healthy ingredients to expand your on-the-road food choices.

<u>WHAT</u> I WAS THINKING: ABOUT SURVIVAL & INGENUITY

When I was a wide-eyed, impressionable juvenile, (why just yesterday, in fact), my mother read a news story of a woman who claimed she was so destitute she had to buy dog food to survive. With all due sympathy to that unfortunate woman, my mother said to me, "There's no reason to buy *dog food*. There are things less expensive and healthier than dog food she could eat. She just doesn't know how to survive."

Watching my mother's example, I learned much about the art of survival and adaptability in the years that followed.

Many years later, that training came in handy (Mom had no idea of the unhealthy extremes to which I would stretch her wisdom). During my senior year in college, I lived on bagels and spring water for a whole summer in order save every penny from my internship income at Con-Edison so that I could buy my first car. (A used Mazda 626, if you must know.)

Even more years later, as an aspiring entrepreneur struggling to make ends meet, I lived with a friend in an apartment in Silver Spring, Maryland. Once, with a total of $1.35 in combined assets to our combined names, and a total of nothing in our combined stomachs, we decided to walk to the nearby Giant Supermarket to buy something to eat. At my suggestion, we came back with a head of cabbage, a small onion, and a pound of brown rice. Using a bottle of soy sauce already in the kitchen, I cooked us a meal that blew his mind. On the days we were lucky enough to be able to afford mushrooms, I showed him how with some diced onions and soy sauce, mushrooms could taste just like meat (we were both vegetarians). I showed him (and could show you, but you'd have to pay me) how to survive on 60 cents a day. Essentially, therefore, I wrote this book to share a few of my own personal survival strategies!

With that said, despite what the visionless "suits" at the publishers think, I present to you: *The CoffeePot Cookbook!*

But, before we go any further: FIRST THINGS FIRST...

I know! I know!

Yes, yes, I know. Technically, this is called an "electric kettle." So sue me. For what should be obvious reasons having to do with my desire to sell huge quantities of this book by giving it a catchy title, I will NOT (nor shall you from now on ever) be referring to this object as an electric kettle. This shall not be *The Electric Kettle Cookbook* (ugh!). I shudder to even think. This, my friends, is a coffeepot.

Hereinafter referred to as "coffeepot"

THE CASE FOR COFFEEPOT COOKING (*It's what's for dinner!*)
Here are a few reasons why coffeepot cooking rocks!

- <u>Quick meals.</u>　　Meals cooked in coffeepots are fast!

- <u>No oil necessary.</u>　There's no oil required. Frying with oils is unhealthy, and I wouldn't suggest you pour cooking oil into a coffeepot. If you wish, you can pour olive oil, or pumpkin seed oil on your meal AFTER it's cooked. I love the taste of pumpkin seed oil over millet!

- <u>No overcooking.</u> Contrary to popular practice and belief, anything that you cook for hours and hours is no longer food.

- <u>No MSG required.</u> Sure, you could cook Ramen noodles 'til the cows come home, and get your lifetime's dosage of MSG, but this is a new paradigm. The theme for the new year is "Reinvention." See Oprah's magazine if you don't believe me.

- <u>Better than Microwaving.</u> Despite what you have been led to believe, microwaving is not cooking. Microwaves change the molecular structure of food, and cause cancer. Most hotels and motels don't offer a microwave anyway!

　　In other words, your coffeepot meals can be dinner. But not the kind of "dinner" you think. Your meals can be DINNER.
D　　Delicious
I　　Instant
N　　Natural
N　　Nutritious
E　　Economical, and
R　　Rejuvenating
　　Based on the above, Coffeepot cooking, (here's where I get deep, and pull something out of the "Wow, There Might Actually Be Something of Redeeming Value in This Book" file) is a metaphor for a new paradigm of eating I call "Rejuven-eating!"

WHAT IS "REJUVEN-EATING?"

Rejuveneating is a way of living, cooking and dining where what you eat heals and rejuvenates your body.

If you want a great book on how to do just that, pick up a copy of *Ideal Meals* by my health advisor, Sasha Poznyak.

Here is the review I wrote for Sasha's book:

"Staying fit, young and healthy is really simpler than most of us have been led to believe. You don't need a medical degree to understand that everything your body ever needs to heal and maintain itself is found in nature, and in the natural foods you eat.

The recipes in Ideal Meals, in their profound simplicity, present delicious meals you and your family will enjoy preparing and eating.

Ideal Meals is also a resource for knowing the exact healing and rejuvenating benefits natural foods provide, and even shows how and when to eat them for optimum effect.

Eat an ideal meal every day, and you'll prevent unnecessary deterioration, address common health issues, remove toxins, balance, normalize and keep your body in an ideal state! And, the best part is: you never need travel any farther than your kitchen!" ~

Walt F.J. Goodridge *[on the vitalityaid.com site]*

But, let's be clear here, that review above is NOT about THIS book. Oh, no. That review is for a REAL health book. What YOU, my dear friend have in your hands at this moment is *The Coffeepot Cookbook*, a whole different cup of tea, or coffee, if you prefer.

However (and here's the tie-in), a real benefit *of The Coffeepot Cookbook* is that you can indeed make some "ideal meals," and rejuveneat" your way to better health! Cool, huh?

But, before we go any further: SECOND THINGS SECOND...

CHAPTER 2
COFFEEPOT BASICS

For nerd coffeepot cooks who need this info to feel warm and cuddly inside.

Electric Ket-, um Coffeepot Basics

At the bottom of the kettle is a sealed electric heating element. Above the heating element is a canister that holds water. The canister can be removable, or it can be built into the kettle. The controls are on the side of the kettle. Typically, there is an on/off switch and a thermostat.

The Heating Element

Coffeepots are powered by a heating element that works in the same way an electric range does. The heating element is a resistor---a material that resists the flow of electricity. When electricity flows into the resistor, it is turned into heat. That heat is what heats up the water inside the coffeepot.

The Thermostat

The thermostat controls the heating element. The thermostat has a variable resistor inside. The higher you set the temperature, the lower the resistance is. A small current runs through the thermostat, controlling an electronic switch called a transistor. The transistor, in turn, controls the heating element. When the resistance goes up in the thermostat, less current flows through, which causes less current to flow to the heating element. When the resistance is reduced, the current through the thermostat increases, which causes the transistor to increase the current through the heating element, raising the water temperature. Blah, Blah, Blah...

TYPES OF COFFEEPOTS *(what to expect in your travels)*

This is my favorite type of coffeepot. The heating coil is hidden in the base of the pot so you get the full interior space to do your cooking. In this particular design, the top of the pot is wide enough to permit some of the, um, things we'll be doing.

This is another popular model found in many hotels. The water is heated by a coil that protrudes into the interior. It is NOT my favorite, only because I worry that the food or other items (stay tuned for that) may be ignited by the coil and burst savagely into flames. Thankfully, this has not happened, and I've been able to cook all the same meals using this type of coffeepot as well.

Can you see the three rings of the heating element at the bottom of the pot? The water actually comes in direct contact with the rings.

If your motel, hostel or budget hotel of choice offers any other type of coffeepot, well, you're out of luck. These are the only two types I've encountered throughout my travels, and thus the only two I shall review here. However, since I'm not a mean person, I'll include some images I googled and grabbed, just so this section can *appear* a bit more comprehensive and researched than it really is.

As you can see, some of these styles of coffeepot have smaller openings at the top or other silly configurations that COULD affect some of the suggestions in this guide. It's a good thing you're adaptable, and enough of a cheapskate to make the best of a little inconvenience if you encounter any of these. Rest assured, however, that the two types I've encountered and reviewed are likely the most economical for small hotels to purchase and provide, so you most likely won't encounter any more sophisticated types in your travels.

The coffeepot cook's worst nightmare: a pot without a top! What were they thinking????

DANGERS OF COFFEE POT COOKING

The range of possible consequences and damage you could inflict on yourself and others by engaging in coffee pot cooking are as wide as the range and scope of idiots worldwide.

On the "*don't sweat the small stuff*" end, you could singe your skin reaching into a hot coffee pot to retrieve a stuck piece of broccoli. (Not too bad.) On the *"Uh-oh, time to get a lawyer"* end, you could cause a fire in your room, that then engulfs the hotel, burns the building to the ground, and ends up cooking not only your rice, but the bodies of countless other hotel guests, causing disfigurement, death, grief and all manner of pain and suffering to them, their families and heirs. (Bad)

Which is not to say that coffee pot cooking is dangerous, mind you. It's no more dangerous than any other form of cooking engaged in with a modicum of common sense. *(If you are right now wondering what the word "modicum" means, then put this book down and ask someone where the nearest restaurant is.)*

DISCLAIMER

That said, I categorically disavow any culpability, responsibility or fault as a result of damages caused by the use of any of the techniques contained in this book. Not only do I hold myself harmless of any responsibility for any damages, but I shall discredit your education, challenge your IQ, cast aspersions upon your upbringing, question your level of sanity, and ridicule you as an individual should I be called upon to testify at any ensuing trial. *(Note to self: If people can sell cigarettes without having to be accountable.....)*

WARNINGS (Having said that, here are some guidelines:)

- do not insert metal objects into a coffeepot
- do not attempt to fry with oil in a coffeepot
- do not leave a coffeepot cooking in a room while you go shopping
- Keep sticky substances away from the heating coils

CHAPTER 3:
What you will need

BASICS

The beauty of coffeepot cooking is that it appeals to the minimalism and frugality (read: cheapness) of its likely practitioners. There are few of these accessories that can't be begged, borrowed or procured by some other means while in your hotel/motel of choice. Here are my suggestions:

1. To eat your food, you will need a knife, fork, spoon, set of chopsticks* or homo-sapien/simian hand with opposable thumb.

2. To serve your food with a modicum of decency, you will need a plate, bowl, empty container or sheet of plastic (You could, conceivably eat directly from the coffeepot using the human or simian hand suggested above, but come on now.)

*Note: This is critical because after much exhaustive research, I've discovered you need at least TWO chopsticks to achieve the desired goal. Any quantity less than two proves frustrating. Spend the money. You can only take cheapness so far. (Zen Buddhism/Existentialism question: what is the sound of one chopstick eating? Answer: the growl of an empty stomach.)

THE TROUBLE WITH STARCH

I did not become a gourmet coffeepot chef overnight. It took a bit of trial and error. Having (successfully, but messily) cooked rice in a coffeepot during a stay at a hotel in Kunming, China, I knew the inherent challenges. The trouble with starchy foods (grains and noodles) is that the residue sticks to metal. So, the next time I embarked on a starchy meal, I knew I had to keep the sticky, starchy grains away from the bottom of the coffeepot or away from the heating coil, if any.

My first idea was to buy a mesh cup that would allow the water but not the grains of rice or millet to pass through.

And it almost worked, too, except that, even though I had measured correctly, I didn't take into account two minor points: (1) the fact that the lid didn't swing all the way back to permit the easy insertion of the mesh cup, and (2) even if it did, the hinge that secured the lid to the coffeepot reduced the opening by a few critical millimeters. So that idea went down the drain [Pun alert!]. What to do?

Note for the terminally cheap: I returned the mesh cup the next day and got my money back. Remember, I was in China, so that's a whole 'nother story and traveler's guidebook on how to return a store-purchased item in China, when you don't communicate well enough to even ask for a receipt. But I digress.

Being China, my next idea was to use a bamboo steamer. However, I didn't believe they actually made coffeepot-sized bamboo steamers, so I didn't bother to look. I needed something flexible. I needed something porous; something that could withstand the heat of the boiling water without leaching chemicals into my food. I needed something re-usable for this, and perhaps other uses. Think, man. Think!!

I've got it! A sock! That's right, a sock! It's porous, flexible, and can be reused for other purposes. Plus I've got a ton of 'em, and it'll be perfect, cause....

....um, wait a minute. That might not go over too well if I invite someone over for a meal, I thought. But, the concept was a good one, and inspired me towards the eventual solution!

So, thus inspired, I headed to the local supermarket in China, and found...drum roll, please....THIS!

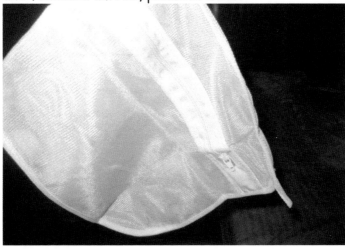

The package says "silk stocking" but we'd call it a small laundry bag. It's advertised as *"great for delicates that get snags on them (silk stockings, etc.) - also for keeping bits together in the wash."*

Perfect! It was definitely flexible, porous, reusable, easy to care for, it had a zipper, the mesh was even smaller than the metal canister, so it would be perfect for smaller grains, AND it was only 5.80RMB (88cents USD). I bought two! (I spare no expense in the interest of fine dining.) Challenge solved.

THE TROUBLE WITH THE BASE

So, the silk stocking baggie solves your challenge with starchy grains. However, you will also need a way to keep the baggie itself away from the interior base of the coffeepot for it, too, may get singed. There are a few ways to do this:

OPTION 1:   It's a little stainless steel tray (that also doubles as garlic holder when I'm not cooking.) **Position it correctly before immersing your baggie into the opening.** (Is it just me, or does that last sentence sound obscene to you, too?)

In any event, you can improvise using anything that you can beg, borrow or procure by other means in and around your hotel. However, whatever you decide to use should not be plastic (which may melt) or glass, (which may shatter in the intense head).

OPTION 2: Rather than placing something <u>inside</u> the pot, you could use a pen, chopsticks, knife, any long tubular object

Shown here is a potato peeler I travel with that works quite well. If your silk stocking baggie has a looped handle like mine does one, you can use it to suspend the baggie away from the bottom of the coffeepot, and also avoid burns when retrieving your baggie if it falls—as it invariably will otherwise—into the boiling water.

Using the suspension method is a better option because any rigid item you buy (option 1), may not be able to fit through the different sized openings of the different types of coffeepots you'll encounter in your travels.

Important: Don't get greedy. Remember, your grains will swell while being cooked. Makes no sense to cook 3 cups of rice and then not be able to pull the now fattened baggie out through the pot opening. Exercise a little self control.

THE TROUBLE WITH LIQUIDS

The other accessory you might need is something to "cook" liquids like sauces and creams. Imagine you have a taste for spaghetti and pasta sauce. You could prepare the spaghetti in your silk-stocking, but what about the sauce? I wouldn't advise boiling it directly in the coffeepot. Things could get ugly.

You'd need something that conducts the heat (i.e. transmits the heat from the boiling water to the sauce), yet something that is also flexible. Any ideas? Raise your hands. Yes, the lady in the back row in the red dress. Yep, ziploc* bag! I knew you'd say that. What are you, on crack??? Just kidding.

In fact, in China, medicinal teas are often provided in plastic bags that are then immersed and heated in hot water before drinking. (Which is not to say this means it's provably safe, but it is, however, commonly done.)

The concerns are (1) the bag may not be intended and designed to withstand the heat of being boiled, and if not, (2) you'll end up eating plastic along with your spaghetti and sauce.

If you're concerned about this, then simply stick (pun alert) with the silk-steamer and bra-baggie recipes and stay away from the plastic-poacher recipes. Surely you can do without spaghetti for the duration of your trip, yes? However, in the interests of optimizing the cooking experience for you, I sought the advice of my health guru, who advised me as follows:

"As long a your ziploc bag does not melt in that boiling water, up to 4 minutes of exposure will not substantially compromise your tomato sauce. You will get some molecules of plastic in there, but not too many. I imagine though, that the bag will start melting in boiling water on the 3rd minute, if not sooner. Why not put a metal container in with the sauce?"

*I use the term "ziploc" in the "xerox," "vaseline," and "fedex" sense to imply ANY generic reusable, re-sealable plastic bag. No suggestion or endorsement of a specific trademarked brand is intended. Blah Blah

So, heeding his advice, I walked around the streets of China, and found this:

 It's called a "dipper," and can be found in any restaurant supply store, reasonably-priced, or jacked up to an exorbitantly high price to take advantage of a visiting foreigner who's too fanatic to eat at a restaurant. But it's perfect. It's stainless steel, and with its long handle, you can insert it into the coffeepot and not suffer third-degree burns attempting to retrieve it when your sauce is done.

Now, <u>your</u> commitment and fanaticism may not run as deeply as mine, and thus you may not want to go to such great lengths to find just the right accessory. Any slim can will do. In fact, you might even be able to use the can the sauce comes in. Or, if you have no self-respect, and don't care what condition you leave your coffeepot for future guests, you could just heat your sauce directly in the pot. This brings me to my next set of suggestions for coffeepot cooking accessories.

OPTIONAL ACCESSORIES:

None of these is essential, but they do make cooking and cleanup just a bit easier, and are not that expensive.

- basin or bottle: to wash your food before preparation.
- cutting board: makes preparation a bit easier and neater
- strainer: to drain the food over the bathroom sink without losing any of your valuable produce.
- sponge: to clean up after yourself.
- steel wool: to remove food that may have burned to the inside of the coffeepot despite my clear instructions.
- sink drain filter: to prevent clogging the hotel plumbing, forcing the management to enter your room to unclog and plunge, risking discovery of your elaborate culinary contraptions and setup. (Again, all of these are optional)

AN ODD WARNING

You may notice, as you read through the book, that the recipes get increasingly elaborate and creative.

As I started to rely more and more on my coffeepot, I started to get more creative, the meals started to get more elaborate and complex. I really started enjoying myself. I'll share with you a little secret. When I made "Curry Carnival," I was staying at a hotel that provided each room with its own coffeepot, but kept a single coffeepot base in the common hallway for guests to use. In order to use your coffeepot, you had to step out into the hallway, place it on the base, boil whatever you wanted to boil, and then return to your room with your coffeepot. They obviously didn't want multiple guests using multiple coffeepots (and electricity) all willy nilly.

Anyway, it was a small hotel, no one else was using the base at 3:00pm when I prepare my meals, so what I did was sneak—um, I mean move the base into my room, use it for the ten minutes it required to prepare my meal, then return the base to the hallway before anyone noticed it was missing! Curry Carnival and all the meals I prepared while at that hotel, were literally stealth meals prepared "on the run" in minutes with only fugitive access to a fully functional coffeepot/base in my room!

Anyway, enough preliminaries! Let's eat!

UM, ALMOST FORGOT

Ohmigosh! The food! I forgot about the food! While this is not a book about shopping, I would be remiss as a coach, consultant, and connoisseur of coffeepot cooking culture and culinary creativity, if I didn't share a few tips on shopping. The advantage of coffeepot cooking is you get to purchase local fruits and vegetables provided you are traveling in an area that has them. Since I often don't have a refrigerator, I only purchase enough for a day's meal. Here's a typical take while I was living in Xishuangbanna, China.

Clockwise from top: almonds, cashews, coconuts, green dates, guava, bokchoy, soy beans, melon, tamarind, scallion, parsley, unknown greens, mangos, rice (bag), garlic

Different day. Same fanatic.

Other than "buy sparingly," I can't offer any other real shopping tips. One thing I *will* say is that so-called "organic" produce in certain developed areas often <u>do</u> have pesticides, while produce in areas where pesticides are expensive, may be less contaminated. Also, in certain cities, you'll need to avoid or accept paying the "foreigner price" for your fruits and veggies. Search my JamaicaninChina.com blog for *"The perpetual pursuit of the perfect, plump, plausibly-priced papaya"* which shows precisely where to find cheap produce in China!

Here's a photo of a meal I need to share with you. Now, in case you're wondering, the object in this photo is not a coffeepot. It's called a wok. This meal was prepared in a wok, on a stove, with a flame. A little bit of oil was used. The exact taste of this meal is NOT one you will be able to replicate effectively in a coffeepot (it'll be close, but not exact). So, why am I showing you this picture? Just to show you I DO actually know how to cook, given different environments. I also show this photo because it may help MY dating prospects at some point in the future, as I've heard women are turned on by men who can cook. This is, after all, all about ME.

You, on the other hand, presumably, since you are reading this book, will be relegated to fend for yourself in the deserted wasteland of culinary options that is coffeepot cooking! (My editor says I should leave that line out, as it may discourage people from "feeling good" about their coffee-pot cooked meals. Blah. Blah. Blah. What does SHE know? She's obviously never gotten as hungry and as desperate as you have, or no doubt will become, once deprived of your familiar cooking options. So, like I said, welcome to the deserted wasteland! Bon appetit!

CHAPTER 4:
RECIPES

Of course, I'm only kidding. Coffeepot cooking is and will be as much fun, and as filling and as flavorful as—and definitely healthier than—regular cooking.

At this point, even if I never shared with you an actual recipe, by simply knowing of the existence of the coffeepot cooking concept, you've already gained some creative insights, and stretched your perception of the possibilities enough to venture out on your own. So, this next section is provided to offer some specific meal ideas and inspiration by showing you some actual, real-life, consumable meals I've prepared, eaten (and lived to talk about) using nothing but a hotel coffeepot and a little ingenuity (mine!)

But before we do, let me share a little caveat (no, not caviar, silly, that would be too expensive for you) about my choice of meals for coffeepot cooking. For me, meals are defined by the starch. When I was growing up in Jamaica, a meal wasn't a meal unless I had rice, or bread, or yams or breadfruit, as "the starch." So, while for some people, the question is, "Where's the meat???" For me, it's "Where's the starch?". The following meals typically include some defining "starch." However, once you master the basics of coffeepot cooking, you can mix and match vegetables (starch or no starch) based on your personal taste. So, now that I've devoted almost half this book to preliminaries and preparation, let's eat!

RECIPE #1: Voracious Veggie Soup
(The original Coffeepot Cookbook blog post that started it all!)

Okay, there's something you need to know about me for when we hang out together for the Jamaican in Russia adventure: I take my diet very seriously. At the same time, I'm not ruled by my gut, at least not the same way other folks are.

So, when I say that I don't eat meat, I don't mean just for today. I mean yesterday, today, tomorrow, the next day, and the day after that. I'm not suddenly going to forget and take the piece of pork you're offering me because YOU forgot that I don't eat meat. (I had a hard time explaining that on a date in Xishuangbanna.) I've been vegan since 1992, so I mean never. It also means I don't eat fish, because last time I checked, fish aren't vegetables.

Also, when I say I'm fasting, I just don't mean "just for right now," and then proceed to take the rice you're offering because it's after 5pm. When I fast, it means I'm not eating.

And when I say I don't eat MSG, or meat flavoring cubes or white sugar or table salt, that's just what I mean.

So, today as I slowly resume eating after my recent seven-day fast, I felt like I wanted something warm rather than the fruits I've been eating for the past 2 days.

However, for reasons I've just stated, I won't eat in a non-vegan restaurant, even though I might request no MSG, no salt, no meat oil, no eggs, etc. I can't be 100% sure that the chef will honor those requests to my satisfaction.

So, today's dish is Walt's Nomad Veggie Soup and noodles from Chapter 7 of the cookbook. [Remember, I wrote this way before this book actually existed]

EQUIPMENT:
- Electric Coffeepot
- Soup bowl (get from front desk)
- Knife
- Spoon
- Empty water bottle

INGREDIENTS: (from local supermarket; grab extra plastic bags while there)
- 4L bottled water
- Rice noodles (optional)
- Bok Choy
- tofu
- scallion
- Garlic
- Ginger
- Sea salt (ordered online)

DIRECTIONS:
Before beginning the process below, note that if you've only got one bowl, you can pour hot water over the dried rice noodles, let soften, remove from bowl, place in hotel teacup, and enjoy as a side dish or include in soup.

Wash bok choy, tofu and scallion with your bottled water. If no basin or pot is available, cut the top off an empty 1.5L or 4L water bottle you've been saving in your room (for just this sort of thing), insert vegetables, pour in water, cover with palm of hand or top half of recently cut bottle, and shake vigorously.

Next, finely dice garlic, ginger and scallion. If no cutting board is available, spread a piece of plastic (the extras you got from the produce section of the supermarket) across the wooden desk of your hotel room. Dice gently, then discard the sheet when done.

• Dice tofu into cubes, Chop bokchoy
• Place diced ingredients, tofu and bokchoy into soup bowl.
• Boil water in coffee pot. Pour water over ingredients in bowl. Cover with plastic sheet or plate. Simmer for a few minutes.
• Stir occasionally.
• Add sea salt to taste.

Voila! Enjoy! (version 1; version 2 with carrots)
(Total prep time: about 10 minutes; EXPENDITURE (RMB):

• tofu: 1.50	• ginger: 0.60
• garlic: 1.20	• water: 10.0
• scallion: 1.70	• noodles: 4.70
• bokchoy: 1.00	

Total cost: 20.70RMB = 3.18US

Next time, we'll make brown rice in a coffee pot. This could get messy. Preparation tip: As most good chefs are aware of and practice, (but I never did until faced with the restrictions of coffeepot cooking), it's a good idea to prepare all your ingredients in advance of actual cooking.

Preparing in advance, means that as my list of ingredients increases, I often need more "dishes" to hold my vegetables and seasonings. However, I suggest to you that coffeepot cooking is inherently more satisfying the more creative and elaborate you

can become in the preparation, and the more conservative and economical you can remain in your overall purchases.*

For the meal shown here, I used some plastic trays that came in some cookies I purchased to wash and ready the ingredients beforehand.

*Did you catch the cool thing I did in matching the elements of that sentence? If not, I'll spell it out for you:

The COFFEEPOT COOKING PRIME DIRECTIVE: Strive always to be
    Creative and Elaborate in Preparation
    Conservative and Economical in Purchases

RECIPE #2: Millet Mountain

This will be your first time using the silk stocking steamer to make a grain-based meal in your coffeepot. Aren't you excited!? I know I am! I'm excited for you! You can adjust

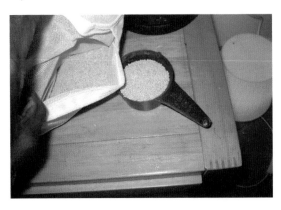

the recipe to include your choice of vegetables. I go with something simple: broccoli and a little parsley. Measure out a cup of millet. (Yes, I always travel with a $\frac{1}{2}$ cup measuring spoon, and you should, too.)

Wash millet (use the silk steamer for this). Cut broccoli into bite-sized crowns. Start water boiling in coffeepot. Immerse and suspend millet baggie in boiling water. Millet tends to absorb water (within the body, too) so

make sure it comes in contact with the water while you're cooking it so that it is not too dry. After 10-15 minutes, your millet should be ready! Fluff to individual preference, serve or eat directly from baggy!

To prepare the broccoli, you can also use another silk stocking to steam it, or you can simply pour hot water over it to blanch.

I also prepared silk-stocking steamed pumpkins for this meal.

You can top your meal with olive oil, (try pumpkin seed oil if you can find it), season it to your unique taste with salt, spices, your favorite condiment (ketchup, sauce, or whatever floats your boat!)

Now wasn't that simple?

As you can see, with just this one innovation, the range of possibilities for meals (while traveling or while on a severely restricted budget) is limitless! You've transformed your coffeepot from an overlooked and underutilized amenity, into a secret source of sustainable meals! Let's continue on our journey to see what else we can cook up!

RECIPE #3: Roamer's Rice

Sometimes, I feel like having a simple meal like brown rice and

vegetables. Using the same technique as Millet Mountain, you can create a brown rice meal fit for a king or queen.

Although healthy and doable, the preparation of brown rice in a coffeepot requires a bit more time, which is why I stick to faster-cooking grains like millet and quinoa. However, variety is the spice of life, so be courageous and with a little patience, you can enjoy Roamer's Rice!

Sprinkle with salt, cayenne pepper flakes and enjoy!

RECIPE #4: Curry Carnival

After much searching for a brand that didn't have MSG, I finally found curry powder in the city I was staying! That opened up new possibilities! Here's my first creation!

INGREDIENTS: Broccoli, pumpkin, dried mushrooms, onions, garlic, ginger, curry powder, cayenne pepper, avocado, yam

PREP: wash vegetables. Soak mushrooms in water for 3 hours, wash again. Slice onions, dice garlic, dice ginger, chop pumpkins, cut broccoli into bite-sized mini crowns. Dishware: Two bowls, two hotel teacup saucers, empty styrofoam tray, steak knife

DIRECTIONS PART 1:

Curry sauce: In a teacup, place sliced onions, garlic, ginger and  (optional) sea salt, sprinkle about two tablespoons of curry over mixture. Boil water in coffeepot. Pour hot water over mixture and mix, crushing onion and garlic to release flavor. Let sit for a while. Add mushrooms and mix some more

Um, I forgot to take a photo of the curry sauce prep stage, but this is what the empty cup looks like! Use your imagination.

DIRECTIONS PART 2:

Silk steam your diced pumpkin and broccoli separately or together. When done, arrange neatly in a bowl or plate (neatness counts, especially if you're having company). Pour your curry sauce over the neatly arranged broccoli and pumpkins, add more garlic, onions and ginger and mushrooms, and then stir it all together and mess it all up carnival style! Avocado, and yams are optional. My yams were bought from a street vendor in China, but could easily have been purchased fresh and then steamed in my own coffeepot.

Here's how mine turned out! Jealous yet? How's yours coming along?

Curry Carnival!

I hope you have as much fun in your coffeepot cooking as I had making these meals. The greatest challenge was finding the patience to take the photos of the meals while resisting diving into them! If you've got the patience, email me your own photos and let's share them with the world!

RECIPE #5: Nomad Noodles

Another great find! Noodles. You might be thinking, "but you were in China, the streets are paved with noodles!" True, but these weren't your average brand of dried noodles for average backpackers, nomads and Chinese nationals. These were wheat-free, vegetarian and advertise "No MSG!" These were fanatic noodles!

In any event, despite the manufacturer's claims, I still didn't use the enclosed packets as they had other suspicious ingredients. I tossed that other junk out and simply ate the noodles. Sometimes I eat them dry, like crackers. I like to have something crunchy in my diet!

So here's the deal. I've found MSG-free curry powder. I've found vegetarian, wheat-free noodles. I've got a hunger for more palate-pleasing meals. And, I've got a magic coffeepot! Stand back, people! It's about to get crazy!

RECIPE #6: Curry Carnival II, the Craze Continues!

With no sea salt, no familiar vegan spices, no msg-free soy sauce, once I got hold of some curry in China, I got so excited, I started currying everything that got close to the coffeepot! I even curried my socks by mistake and had to throw them out. But I digress. The next day, I curried broccoli, carrots, mushrooms, much the same as before, except this time, I added the noodles! The recipe, therefore, is pretty much the same, but the end result, however....eat your heart out!

The culinary coffeepot curry-cooking craze continues!

RECIPE #7: Tin Can Tortellini*

The alternate name for this recipe is Ziploc Zitini, both of which have nothing to do with what the recipe is really about, which is, in fact, simply spaghetti and pasta sauce. However, as you'll no doubt agree, *Ziploc Zitini* and *Tin Can Tortellini* are in fact, cool names, while soup can spaghetti is not. In any case, you can use this technique to create any pasta/sauce combination of your choice. With that said, here's how to make spaghetti in a coffeepot!

DIRECTIONS:
Break your spaghetti sticks into thirds. This is important so that they will fit inside the silk stocking steamer. Immerse and boil your spaghetti to the desired consistency.

SAUCE OPTION 1:
Place an adequate amount of sauce into your dipper, bring the water in your coffeepot to a boil, and place the dipper into the pot until sauce is heated to desired temperature.

SAUCE OPTION 2:
Bring your water to a boil. Insert plastic bag of sauce for no more than 3 minutes.

Or, just go for it!

If you decide that all of the above breaking and dipping and zipping and locking is too much hassle and you just want to go for it, here's my advice. Throw the whole kit and kaboodle into the coffeepot and let it boil! Stir continuously to reduce the sticking. There's no way to adjust the heat like you would on a stove, so you might try switching off, unplugging or removing the coffeepot from the base to moderate the heat. Let me know how it goes. Or, actually, please don't mention or implicate me in any way on this. You're on your own.

*Why no photo? Well, I don't like spaghetti, actually.

RECIPE #8: Striver's Strings

For today's dish, I was experimenting with some ingredients I don't typically eat a lot. Radishes and celery aren't on my usual list of choices. However, I wanted to live true to my decision to eat a more raw food diet. Most of the ingredients can actually be eaten raw, and so don't require a lot of boiling or steaming. Note, this meal was actually prepared before I found the curry powder, so it isn't is colorful as the previous one!

INGREDIENTS:
millet, string beans,
celery, radish,
garlic, pumpkin

Silk-steamed millet

pot boiled pumpkin

blanched string beans
with pepper flakes

almost raw celery, garlic
and radish

RECIPE #9: Fantastic Flavorful Fruit Fiesta

Perhaps the easiest coffeepot cookbook recipes are those that don't need a coffeepot. Ha! Seriously, though, remember that "rejuveneating" is about eating healthfully. Eating a constant diet of cooked food is not good for you. Fresh, uncooked, raw, ripe produce is essential for good health.

Papaya and longan

Papaya and cherries

Mango and rambutan
note to self: take photo before eating.

Watermelon

Okay, I admit, I DID use my coffeepot to wash the fruit, although washing the melon was a bit tricky...

RECIPE #10: Tofu Temptation

What kind of vegan would I be if I didn't include an ode to tofu in the form of a coffeepot cooked meal?

INGREDIENTS: tofu, greens, millet, bean sprouts, avocado, yam

The yams for this meal, too, were purchased already steamed by a street vendor. You, too, should feel free to incorporate pre-cooked as well as coffeepot-cooked components into your meals to add some variety and flavor!

RECIPE #11: Cashew, Carrot, Cayenne (& Curry) Cacophony

It's becoming frightfully obvious that at some point I will be forced to end this book as the list of ingredients and the complexity of these coffeepot meals increases... and I run out of cutesie alliterative names for them!

INGREDIENTS
Avocado, scallion, tofu, garlic, carrots, millet, broccoli, cashews, ginger, curry, cayenne pepper

Don't be intimidated by the complexity of the meals. Just take one step at a time and you'll be fine.

RECIPE #12: Sweaty Summer Salad

Don't like the name of this dish? Well, I'll have you know that sweat is a good thing! Sweating keeps the body purged of toxins. But lest you get worried, I'm not suggesting that you use sweat (yours or someone else's, in the literal sense) as an ingredient in your salad, although, now that I think about it....Anyway, I digress. The salad "sweats" when you pour hot water (courtesy of your magic coffeepot) over it mainly just to clean it. Even though my diet leans towards the raw, in some areas I travel, I avoid eating uncooked greens just for sanitary reasons. I wash them, and then wash them again with some hot water.

Broccoli, Carrots & A Sweaty Salad (parsley, bokchoy, that other thing with the fat stalk; The avocado and tomatoes not warmed.)

RECIPES #13 TO INFINITY!

As I've said, once you get the hang of coffeepot cooking, the combinations and permutations are endless!

The process is simple. Make the millet or rice first (i.e. the item(s) requiring the longer cooking time), then cover and set aside.

Wash the coffeepot interior, and start with fresh water for each separate item that you steam or blanch. Here are a few photos of meals I've created, and that you can too!

Millet, pumpkin, greens, avocado

Mushrooms, cashews noodles in curry sauce

Asparagus & mushrooms,

Avocado on the side sprinkled with sea salt

Cashews, cauliflower, greens

Avocado, tomato, yams

CONCLUSION

Well, there it is! Coffeepot Cooking: an idea whose time has come! A revolution in thought for the new millennium! A monumental paradigm shift that challenges centuries of dogma and shakes the core of civilization to its very foundations! Um, or at the very least, a quirky little idea of how to cook in a coffeepot.

However, you define it, I hope you've enjoyed what may hopefully be the first in a long, continuing, world famous series of coffeepot cookbooks! Before I send you on your way to conquer the world with what you've learned, here are a few more important ideas, new findings and suggestions! (And remember, send photos of your finished meals to me at meals@coffeepotcookbook.com!) Enjoy, and....

....Eat well and prosper!

CHAPTER 5:
Good ideas

THE NATURAL NOMAD'S COMBINATION SPICE RACK AND FIRST AID KIT

Hippocrates is credited with saying, *"make your food your medicine, and your medicine your food."* The rest of that famous quote is actually: *"...or you won't get any dammed dessert!"* See, it was actually Hippocrates' <u>mother</u> who uttered those now famous words to get him to eat his vegetables. However, there is truth behind what mother Hippo said.

If you are embarking on this worthwhile adventure into coffeepot cooking, there are some spices that will enhance the flavor and taste of your meals while providing tremendous preventive, healing and rejuvenative benefits all at the same time. It's like having a spice rack and a first-aid kit in one!

Sea salt: supplies essential minerals

Cayenne: improves circulation; kills bacteria and viruses, helps remove dead cells, improves metabolism

Turmeric: anti-parasitic; anti-inflammatory, tissue-restorative

Cloves: kills parasites, raises serotonin levels improving mood

Garlic: enhances immunity, kills bacteria and viruses, assists in digestion and elimination

Ginger: anti-inflammatory, improves kidney function and helps dissolve kidney stones

EXTRASSENTIALS: If you're traveling the world and dining in establishments of dubious hygiene and eating foods of unknown origin, purity, cleanliness, preparation technique and ingredients, there are few items you should have in your luggage.

Zinc: kills bacteria, enhances brain function

Oil of oregano: kills bacteria

Tea tree oil: kills bacteria and molds

Chlorophyll: Detoxifying, provides micronutrients for metabolic processes

Vitamin C: Antibacterial; enhances cellular metabolism

DRAT! BUT WE LIVE AND LEARN

An advantage, and one of the selling points of *The Coffeepot Cookbook* is that there is no dismantling or disabling necessary. And that is still true….um, until it's not.

I had recently changed hotels and while I was scouting out the room, was pleased to note that there was indeed the perfect coffeepot (no heating coil; smaller diameter opening, but still bigger interior volume) in the room. Encouraged by this, I booked the room forthwith, content that I would thus be able to continue my writing, creation, experimentation and completion of *The Coffeepot Cookbook.*

Imagine my horror and surprise therefore, when, upon opening the lid of the coffeepot to prepare my first meal at the new location, I encountered THIS:

Yes, not one, but count 'em two obstructions in the opening: a little chin-up bar and a plastic filter attachment. It was eerie. It was almost as if the hotel

Egad! Drat, and double drat!!

management somehow knew I was writing this book, knew what I was planning to do in their hotel, and THEN commissioned the creation of a special coffeepot, placed a bulk order, had them delivered overnight from somewhere in China, installed them in all the rooms, all in the three days between when I first booked the room, and when I actually moved in, all with the express and deliberate intention of thwarting my objectives and the creation of *The Coffeepot Cookbook*. (Um, you don't think I'm being too paranoid, do you?)

In any event, much to my elation, I discovered that those two evil obstructions to freedom-loving coffeepot cooks everywhere, and their feeble attempt at preventing fine dining in the world's hotels, actually snap out (and back in) quite easily, providing unfettered access to the coffeepot interior the way God intended it should be. Power to the people!!

But what we've learned from this, boys and girls, is that there's a &(&(*% conspiracy against us—um, no, what I meant to say is we've learned that these types of coffeepots do exist, but with just a teensie, weensie little bit of disabling, will be good to go. Just remember to snap the little bar and the little filter back in place before you check out.

We don't need no stinkin' filters or chin-up bars

WHEN GOOD IDEAS GO HORRIBLY WRONG
(or, "The road to hell is paved with used coffeepots")

This book could change everything. *The Coffeepot Cookbook* could change the game as we know it. Let me explain.

On the *"good-for-them-not-so-good-for-you"* side, hotel owners, realizing they've been missing out on a potential revenue stream, and that their rinky-dink accommodations and bare bones amenities have the capacity to create an elegant dining experience, may start to advertise their rooms as "coffeepot equipped" and charge you more! It could happen!

On the *"bad-for-them-even-worse-for-you"* side, hotel owners, aware that my little exercise in creative cooking, if practiced by increasing numbers of people, could raise their insurance risk and thus their premiums, and thus your daily rate, could spearhead a coffeepot cooking backlash the wrath of which the service industry has never seen. There could be signs like this posted in every hotel lobby throughout the world!

This would not be good.

So, my point is this: while you have every right to steam a carrot in your room using your coffeepot, without needing to sign a release form, or securing FDA or government permission. If I were you, I wouldn't share this book with anyone who works in hotel management, or show up at the check-in counter with a dog-eared copy of *The Coffeepot Cookbook* in your hand.

WHEN GOOD IDEAS GO REMARKABLY WELL
(or, "It doesn't get any better than this!")

On the other hand, this could be the start of something big and revolutionary!

On the *"good-for-you-even-better-for-me"* side, by purchasing this book, millions of backpackers across the world would save money, and eat healthily, and I would receive all the praise, as well as my fair share of wealth as a result.

On the *"good-for-you-not-so-good-for-me"* side, millions of backpackers across the world would save money, eat healthily, buy SHARING the book on social networks, peer-to-peer sites and email, and I would receive all the credit, but NOT my fair share of wealth as a result. That would suck, but would not be unexpected when one writes a book targeted to the chronically or situationally cheap.

On the *"gooder-for-me-who-gives-a-crap-about-anyone-else"* side, I could make the New York Times and Amazon bestseller lists as a result of my great idea and superb writing skills! My point, therefore, is you should (and force your friends as well to) buy the &$^#*# book. It's fourteen stinkin' dollars!

This would be good.

ABOUT THE AUTHOR

Once upon a time, there was an unhappy civil engineer living in New York, who hated his job. More than anything else, he simply wanted the freedom to live true to his self. So, he followed his passion, started a series of sideline businesses, made enough money to quit his job, escaped the rat race, ran off to a tropical island in the Pacific, and created a tourism business so he could give tours of the island to pretty ladies every day and see the world. He now lives his happily reinvented, dream life as a "nomadpreneur" somewhere in a land far away....and writes about it in the award-nominated "Jamaican in China" blog. At this very moment, he's probably preparing and about to eat a delicious coffeepot-cooked meal!

WALT'S BOOKS (available at www.passionprofit.com)

Turn Your Passion Into Profit
The Tao of Wow
The Ageless Adept
Change the Game
This Game of Hip Hop Artist Management
Life Rhymes for the Passion-Centered Life
Come into Our Whirl
Lessons in Success
Hip Hop Profits
The Hip Hop Record Label Business Plan
The Niche Market Report
Jamaican on Saipan
Chicken Feathers and Garlic Skin
Doing Business on Saipan
Living True to Your Self
The Coffeepot Cookbook
Harlem to Hainan (coming soon!)

Learn more about Walt at www.waltgoodridge.com and watch for updates at www.coffeepotcookbook.com